Into This Sea of Green: Poems from the Prairie

poems by

Janet McMillan Rives

Finishing Line Press
Georgetown, Kentucky

Into This Sea of Green: Poems from the Prairie

ACKNOWLEDGMENTS

Called to Stay, The First Red Leaf, The Poet's Hand, New Providence, and
Markers appeared in various issues of *Lyrical Iowa* (1990-2017).
In the World and At the Sandoz Place appeared in *Against the Grain* (1988).
Amish Roofers appeared in *The Blue Guitar* (2018).
Our Little Coal of Fire and Like a String on my Finger appeared in
Sandcutters (2016, 2017).
Triple Moon Shot, Through the Sandhills, New Highways, and Shade Garden
Greens appeared in *The Avocet* (2016-2018).
Sandhills Wildflowers and Memorial appeared in *Voices from the Plains I*
(2017).
Maintaining a Prairie and First Snow appeared in *Voices from the Plains II*
(2018).
The Trees Tell the Story appeared in *Heartsong* (1990).
No Caboose appeared in *Fine Lines* (2018).
Frigid appeared in *The Weekly Avocet* (2017).

To members of my Iowa writing group (The Wordies), special thanks for
your comments and encouragement over the years.

Publisher: Leah Huete de Maines
Editor: Christen Kincaid
Cover Art and Design: Kim Sosin
Author Photo: Darin Wallentine

Order online: www.finishinglinepress.com
also available on amazon.com

Author inquiries and mail orders:
Finishing Line Press
P. O. Box 1626
Georgetown, Kentucky 40324
U. S. A.

Table of Contents

In memory of my parents
Sam and Louise McMillan

Called to Stay

*"My field unamplified as the voice
of one bird's in the corn...." Mona Van Duyn, "Falls"*

I would have settled
for the single crop,
would have been thrilled
to drive the curvy road
past the Quaker meeting house
past the horse farm
around the bend
where the red tailed hawk
soared above the trees
left twisted by the spiral wind.

The place you left
is like the place I left,
the place from which I was taken
on great adventures,
from which I was torn, finally,
from my moorings
till so much later I dropped anchor
into this sea of green
and heard your bird
call me to stay.

The First Red Leaf

Still summer, yet today
the first red leaf has fallen
from an Amur maple
it seems.

Its seams barely dent
the garnet skin.
Black specks
abound.

Around the edge
jagged peaks prick
saying: stay away,
leave me be.

Leaf,
rest here.
Welcome fall
where you fell.

In the World

On D-35 in Hardin County
about midway between the two places
where I know people,
a tractor approaches from the north
driven by a boy of about thirteen.

I feel a kinship of space and time
with this young man I've never met.
We share the sky
in the canvas my windshield frames
and the roadside ditches
left unmowed for the pheasants.
We own the fields
in greens and tans
and other greens again,
his the ownership by deed
if he should choose in years to come,
mine the momentary possession
by eyes and heart in passing.

We are in the world together
my young farmer friend and I,
sharing this split second of being
on a county blacktop somewhere.
That's reason enough for a wave I think.
So does he.

At the Sandoz Place

It takes a hard place to soften the heart.
It takes icy nights to melt the soul,
a heavy door closed against the cold
to open you up enough to let the stranger in,
sharing the darkest secrets life has left you.

It takes the searing summer sun to cool your fire,
the relentless wind to calm your pace
and make you stop and look and love this land,
love it into what you want it to be,
something green and growing
something that will last forever.

It takes hills that roll along
in perfect space, without a tree
to make a man put in the seed
to make him try and fail, time after time
till now the fruit abounds, falls to the ground,
an orchard in all its glory
too few will ever see.

Markers

So small, so gray
they nearly disappear
against the winter white,
the leaden sky.
It takes two trips
at least to even notice
the ragged rows of barren squares,
another two and spring
to make the connection
between these markers
and the County Home up the hill
a safe cornfield away.

Whose place do you mark?
Whose soul do you guard
against the passing stranger
asking to know whose life this was?

Stand your ground. Protect.
No one needs to know
whose heart you hold.

New Providence

It's been a year since the wind twisted through here
a year to the month maybe even to the day.
I've often thought about this place since then
about how suddenly it must have happened
a minute, maybe two, just time enough
to turn around and watch it blow away.

Perhaps you've felt this too
losing something, someone so quickly
you hardly have the chance to be frightened.
Then the storm blows over
and you're left alone like these trees
torn and twisted in such a way
you can never get quite straight again.

The Poet's Hand

for James Hearst (1900-1983)

You must have left just as I arrived,
out the back door as I came in the front.
Funny that no one told me.
No one mentioned a word about what you saw
about what you had to say.
Strange that not one person
put a book in my hand and said: Read.
He will tell you about this place.
He will teach you more than you could learn
in a lifetime here.

I found you on my own
found you standing on this dark earth
a part of the landscape.
I saw you under the honeysuckle branches,
came across you in the attic, below the clock tower,
in a house on that elmless street.

More than once I have felt your hand on my shoulder,
sensed a nudge ever so slight.
I have heard you whisper: Go ahead and try.
You too can see this world with words.

Amish Roofers

We see them all over town after the hail storm,
carried by van from their farms, too far away
for horse and buggy of the Old World Amish.
They answer my morning greeting with   *hello,*
cute puppy dog   just a slight German accent.

Each Amish congregation must decide
what to accept of our modern ways.
These men have accepted little.
Their clothing is plain and humble: bright blue shirts,
buttoned pants, suspenders, straw hats.
Most are clean shaven, unmarried,
or bearded, married. No mustaches, though,
too militaristic for these pacifists.

Be ye not conformed to this world they are taught.
Yet here they are among us
doing what they learned at home.
I watch them work, converse, laugh,
brother with brother, friend with friend,
impressed that these men have met a goal
beyond my reach: they've held back time.

Our Little Coal of Fire

A cinnabar crystal hides in pine,
a cardinal perhaps. But no,
this bird is a glowing ember,
a vermilion flycatcher
who's wandered from the desert
to thrill us with his brilliance.

It's as if we survived the cold
wet summer for this day alone,
for the long lost southwest wind
bending corn still in the fields,
carrying Indian summer and our bird
on his trip north.

It seems we've waited months
for this one moment of beauty
beyond our everyday expectations,
beyond the russet glow of a hawk's tail,
the burnished orange of a robin's breast.

This single spark of scarlet,
our *brasita de fuego*, calls to us
peet-a-weet, peet-a-weet,
and sends us off on our annual journey
through days of gray and beige.

Restoration

*First prize, Exterior Rehabilitation, One-Ten,
One-Twelve Linden Street, Camden.*

The row house is like so many
I walked past, day after day,
            abandoned
so far inside myself, I could never
see green glass among the cinders,
could never imagine the promise
of repointed brick, pine colored
posts, rich cream trim.
I saw only cinders, rotted wood,
peeling paint, rats.

Escape
to prairie and cornfield,
a mosaic of lapis, amber, jade
seasons of renewal.

Triple Moon Shot

We head out for an evening drive
along Sowbelly Road,
twisting, turning, tracing W
and then J as we follow the creek
winding north through pine hills.
Above, a golden escarpment
is lit by the waning sun.

What seems to be a dead gopher
becomes, instead, a snapping turtle,
very much alive, laying eggs
in the burrow she has dug
smack dab in the middle of our track.

Down the road, we stop the car
to see the sun's remaining rays
cast a purple glow on rugged rocks.
Then facing east, surprise,
we see an ivory disc rise.
Three shutterbugs, enraptured
        click, click, click.
The full moon, captured.

First Snow

Fat flakes falling quietly
at the pace of a poem
landing on big
billowing pine boughs.
Snow, soft as a pillow,
fresh as an unrumpled
coverlet of white cotton.

Maintaining a Prairie

To manage a wildflower prairie,
a controlled burn is recommended.

      I will be careful, though,
      to save something from the past.

Fire promotes plant growth, keeps down
spotted knapweed, recycles nutrients.

      We can renew the living part of soil
      with oxygen, hydrogen, nitrogen, carbon.

Burning in April or early May
helps warm-season prairie plants.

      I will choose a day that smells like dirt,
      a day that cries renewal.

Burning is quite effective but wait until
the third year after planting your prairie.

      We can abide leafy spurge that crowds out
      phlox, beardtongue, milkweed, memories.

Burn only part of your prairie each year
to foster survival of over-wintering insects.

      I will shelter people, days, places
      knowing the best will come back.

The Trees Tell the Story

They line what must have been the drive
leading to the house no longer there.
Like old men caught in the open
they reach out to grab something
that will steady their balance
as the wind catches them
this day on the brink between winter and spring.

In another season, another time,
these trees rustled in the summer breeze.
They anchored the cord that held the clothes,
suspended the swing that sailed the little girl
to faraway dreams.
They shaded the aunts, uncles, cousins
setting off for home after a sunny Sunday dinner.

Exactly what happened here?
What hard edge of life
cut the heart out of this place,
cut the ties that bind man to land?
What made this family want to leave
these trees to grow alone?
Perhaps they simply had it
with the struggle, so they left.
They left and never looked back.

If you choose to hide what has happened,
protect your past,
by all means, knock down the house,
burn the boards, bury the bricks.
But don't forget the trees
for they will tell your story.

No Caboose

An orange bullet blasts across the Sandhills
on an iron path traveled by so many early trains.
The letters *BNSF* leap off the engine's side,
Burlington, Northern, Santa Fe
reminiscent of lost lines: Mississippi Railroad,
Central Pacific, Chicago and Northwestern.

Farmers, ranchers, immigrants.
Mr. Shimerda arrived from Prague clutching his violin,
heart already broken by the stark landscape.
Anna Sedlacek boarded an orphan train
bound for Pawnee, Nebraska
where she stood on the stage of the opera house
waiting for a new family to claim her.
Hobos rode these rails during the Depression,
looking for work anywhere. A decade later
young soldiers headed to coasts
not knowing what dread lay ahead.

Belongings, grain, war goods,
baby blue Fords from Detroit, cherry red Toyotas
going east, trailers-on-flat-cars
ready to be transformed into semis on interstates.
Now trains bulge with black nuggets.
Coal trains run east from Powder River basin.
Coal cars completely empty on their return
bring nothing to Wyoming ranchers.

And after the coal is gone from wind blown
pitted high plains, what then?
No engineer gazes at rolling hills of purple lupine,
no horn bellows at a single passing car.
Only white blossoms of field bindweed
embellish ungroomed ballast.

Connected

to this place that sheltered me
nurtured me
let me go.

Connected as to an old friend
familiar, secure
a welcoming landscape.

Connected to evolution
the unexpected
a rush of hidden water.

Connected to ancient seas
mixed grass prairie
moored dunes.

Connected to Nebraska.

Sandhills Wildflowers

Here's what I saw:

    Scarlet gaura
       Hood's phlox
          Purple lupine
             Creamy soapweed
         American vetch
      Showy milkweed
    Scarlet globemallow.

Here's what I'll remember:

    Bright white pendants
       on a twining choke chain—
         Field bindweed.

Tattered

Streets with store fronts
        boarded
no women walking
        no high heels clicking
no men talking
        no pipe smoke drifting.

Farmsteads gone
        wood rotted
just foundations
        mortared stone
hint at creaking
        floorboards under foot.

Photographs
        long faded
high school sweethearts
        disappeared
nearby neighbors
        out of sight.

Remnants.

Like a String on my Finger

The barely audible click
my watch makes
every hour
reminds me to start again
fresh with wonder.

    click

I focus on what I see
    the cloud
      the pine
        the jay.

    click

I dwell for a moment
on what I hear, taste, feel.
Each hour I'm clicked
into thinking about
the little things we notice

    click

the big things we come to.

Through the Sandhills

We drive west, keeping pace
with an empty coal train
under an uncluttered sky,
the earth, too, almost barren.
Even the towns seem sparse—
Ashby, Bingham, Ellsworth, Lakeside—
not much to them.

The land between takes on
a calming shade of green
reminding me of Capulin volcano
a place where I found peace.
Forest greens appear
along streams and hedgerows
punctuating a landscape
so subtle.

Even my mind becomes
uncluttered
set free from worries, choices.
And my heart? Overflowing
taking all this in.

God, it is gorgeous.

New Highways

The lilacs, sturdy from years without pruning,
huddle together. With branches intertwined
they shiver against the morning's icy stillness.
By afternoon the wind will be up
shaking the nest that sits securely now
cradled in leafless lilac arms.
In this suspended moment
the late rising sun spreads itself wider,
now orange now pink now blue.
What a winter picture: nest, bare branches, sunrise.

But here comes the transitory nature of life
cutting the season's solitude with its distractions:
the sound of motors running cold and hard
the blur of colored metal moving on concrete.

Where is the safety of emptiness now?
Where is the radiant beginning of day?
Where is the sunrise?

Autumn Reds

A crayon palette paints the day
from the bittersweet glow of fall's first fire
to the deep maroon of cherry leaves
hanging on past all the rest.

Orange-red crabapple berries stop the birds
in their tracks and sedum, just yesterday
a faint pink buzz, today is darkened
to a regal, bee-free magenta.

Violet-red snapdragons stand May-strong
against Virginia creeper
already gone from summer green to brick red,
the unmistakable sign of what is coming.

Above it all, red-topped maples
share the autumn heights with
white clouds and blue sky in a simple
patriotic gesture to the season.

Memorial

They've been gone for some time now,
packed it in who knows when,
left the farm just as it was.
No son, then, to toil from dawn to dusk,
no sister's son, no daughter's husband.
They left it empty, abandoned.

But here the iris still bloom.
On a Monday in late May
these strong sentries stand at lane's end
supporting the blossoms that catch
the eye of a passing motorist,
a pink-purple memorial
to those who worked the fields
as long as they could,
never imagining ethanol
or today's price of corn.

Frigid

Minus five
feels like minus fifty-one
feels like icicles
in your nose
like cubes between your toes.

Winds from the northwest
at thirty miles an hour
feels so cold it's hot
like an iron on your face
like a walk in outer space.

Snow blowing
every which way
feels like you're smothering
like you can't see ahead
feels like you're already dead.

Shade Garden Greens

I need a box of forty-eight Crayons to name
the greens I see here in the shade garden.
There is grass green spread out before us,
dark pine green of the arborvitae,
double greens of the variegated hosta,
blue green on the inside yellow green on the edge
and the reverse, cream on the inside
tipped in a deep sea green.
There is spring green of ferns
and—surprise!—the exact same shade
in the birch tree's leaves. The birdhouse with
its mint green roof hangs above big and little
double green hosta. And the light green garden shed
with its sage green door awaits the gardener who uses
her apple green thumb to create this tonal magic.

J anet McMillan Rives was born in Hartford and raised in Storrs, Connecticut. In high school she moved to Tucson, Arizona where she currently lives. She is a graduate of the University of Arizona (B.A.) and Duke University (M.A., Ph. D.). She taught college economics for thirty-five years and retired as Professor Emerita of Economics from the University of Northern Iowa. In addition to writing, her interests include travel, gardening, and golf.

Her love of poetry began during her youth in New England when she discovered the poetry of Robert Frost. She has been reading poetry her entire life and actively writing poetry since the late 1980s. Among her favorite poets are W. S. Merwin, Ted Kooser, Mary Oliver, Naomi Shihab Nye, and Ofelia Zepeda. In addition to being active in small poetry writing groups, she was a member of the Iowa Poetry Association when living in Iowa and is currently a member of The Arizona State Poetry Society and the Tucson Poetry Society. Her poems have appeared in *Lyrical Iowa, Ekphrastic Review, Sandcutters, The Avocet, Unstrung, The Blue Guitar, Fine Lines* and in the anthologies *A Song of Myself, Variations of White, Bittersweet, Against the Grain, Heartsong, Voices from the Plains, Facing West,* and *Desert Tracks: Poems from the Sonoran Desert,* and *The Very Edge.* This is her first collection of poetry.